Hate & the Love

Someone almost shot me.
Cops want to stop me.
I'm getting too comfortable.
I stay with a pack like launchable.
Militant movement off me
Sounds funny when you come up.
Too fast
It has to add up when you doing the math
On something horses with six legs
Cheetahs with rabbits above they head.
Estranged with the bed.
Just visas in charisma inhibiters.
Under minding worlds meant for the dead
I see it all then I don't.
That feeling when you woke.
Stepped in and subjected.
To more than what you know.
Dark as the back of my neck
Its easy to let it go.
Messages injected.
Suddenly swaying you in the decision

In your vote
Fuse make them loose they shoes.
So many new dudes
Can't tell who's who.
Who knows why the lord?
Do what he do.
Just hope he don't choose you.
Try to imagine where I was at
When shit was like that
When they used to holla get em Black
Not out the streets yet
Still got to watch my back.
Made it further than expected.
Still and never telling.
Silence is a investment.
You can always see this life's lesson.
A lot of fake promises during election
We see the difference in seats.
Where our reality meets
And nothings getting better.
Grateful but any day It can be me.
And still overpaying for shelter
We are dying a feet away this is my letter
To whomever

The road less traveled the words hardly spoken.

The wiped away tears without notice.

The voices unheard

The pain and the scars

Bottled up emotion of the Hate & the love

What you Think

For me its metabolic
Just can't part with
The ultra-sonic
A compartment
Down to the atomic
Get lost in the world like it was abolished.
By something catastrophic
Sandpaper thoughts to the rawest
Until I'm lethargic
Tongue tapered suited for the logic.
Exercise the principles like it was CrossFit.
Right of passage can you handle the action.
The corner is where your back is.
How deep is your commitment.
Mixing artistic with the mistic
See if its that real shit we going to hear it.
Land where the dead is living.
Plenty pots but no food in the kitchen
Only dishes for the ones putting work in
Breed mask and glove antics
Where money ends the best of friendships
Family forgets your relatives.

Function paranoia its all on a different metric
Desperate measures
Everyone got a gun for the leverage.
Its really like a western
Won't skip a beat from the noise.
But got a jump shot.
Hoping you get far.
Settle for cars gold
And ladies with a Fashionova budget
Respect and hate fluctuate.
No steady pace trying to find a way.
Trust don't integrate.
Only common comradery
Is the green than we inhale.
Help my feelings calibrate.
Using the platform to ventilate
Debate how to fall in place.
Night that I stay awake and contemplate.
Separate keeping my distance safe.
Honor in persuasion
Master in paper getting.
Doctoring in the current
Mic diplomacy
These are my proudest days.

I can't give it all away.
What you think you getting from me
Where were you when shit was ugly?
I know you never loved me.

By any means

Get from around me your too close.

You leave me with no choice.

I'm the new voice.

No cap

Just facts

Conception to the hoist

Elevate with the noise.

Racketeering everyone got a hustle

mine different than yours.

Same reasoning behind doors.

Portals cut from fits off floors.

We leave impressionable prints then stored.

Characterized styles that breed encores.

They are watching and they need more.

The drought just a liquidation to prepare for the new draw.

Lottery winning number start to form.

Organizing arrangements like world tours

Payroll ready to separate physical and spiritual like chores.

Lawyers save lives,

like they were sent from the lord.
How can I ever be bored.
With age come wisdom,
might not ever move if you stop,

Vows

I'm what you call that good love.
Leg twitching rip the pillow love.
She wants all the time.
I'm something like a good drug.
Straight to the buckle
Cause the thought of me makes her form a puddle.
I can't front she got all that I want.
Thick lips thick thighs
Nice face and pretty eyes
I whisper in her ears, and she licks mine
Skin glowing in the candlelight.
Taking my time to make it feel right.
One hand on her tits she is biting her lips.
Digging diving swimming
She pulls me over.
And moans louder as her climax get closer.
Faster I fast
Deeper I go deep.
Smack her on her ass.
Then I ask whose it is
She screaming black.

Thrashing drowning in her waters
From the top to the edge
Falling off the bed
She grinds her hips.
It was worth the kiss.
Put on a show for this.
She says she loves my dick.
She a freak and I noticed it.
Pandoras box I opened it.
Hand cuffs locked doors don't open it.
Gummy bear nipples
Call her titti luscious.
Dark skin ghetto
Wears blond braids.
Roll my blunts after a long day
Gives bomb brain.
From down south
Only thing she scared of is hurricanes.
Try to warn me she's a soaker.
Sharing secrets late night over strip poker
Showed her who I really am.
Loose change crumble bills in my pants
Counting future money by the gram
Stacking green like I like

Pickles with my relish

Extra clips with my weapons

Wants me to put in best and feel it all.

With prejudice

Fuck her without protection.

I think she got a fetish.

She is making channel and Gucci vows.

I order pounds for that walk around.

She my down

Waited for the right one to come to town.

I'm the only one to release her of those contained sounds.

Black on black drop

Paraphernalia through the top

High speeds she doesn't want me to stop.

Out 4 Control

**Blunt hit like memory foam
it remembers your spot.
Key lock
Position progress
Precision vision
And still with the scissors
Under my sleeves to cut the tight knots
Money the only friend I need to keep me young.
Plays don't stop every play a avenue of trust.
Listed transactions.
Even in your passing it never releases us.
It likes to know who we are.
See your way up your way to the top.
Envision the lift pull your way up.
Until you are who you are.
Fuck it I might let a clip go.
If he glances and act like he know.
Stand my ground,
like fighter that don't move his feet when he boxes.
Fuck with those women,
that get them checks and card popping.**

They take me out shopping.

Got to be foreign for them to hop in

The only car I get topped in

Hire them to cut the coke.

They done gone wild the way they walk around topless.

Come on

This shit gonna blow like muffler of a 84.

You don't got to know to know

But if you don't

I'm in the hot tub Champaign drinking.

Top floor presidential living

I don't know where I'm going,

But I'm chilling in white lien.

Two bad ones with me

Stripping and kissing

Now tell me what I'm missing.

I got to be the image

I need to be stress free.

With something like a Martha Stewart in the kitchen

These are more than just wishes.

The Bae to the Jay

The Bonnie to the Clyde

The misses above all the mistresses

Forgive me for my times being dismissive.

Extra explicit

All that I'm doing is giving.

Reup and then flip it.

The cycle of business

Go where it takes no brakes on the go.

Baggies to boxes

Cars into boats

Washingtons now Franklins

I'm out for control.

Who am I

I'm hanging on like a thin thread.
Bullets in the chamber
A slight movement of my finger on the trigger
and you dead
do before done to you.
or end up in a pine.
on the corner
where they pronounced you a goner
they place their shrines.
nowhere to go repetitive shots
your stomach in knots
show no mercy like a suicide bomber
if I go then, you go.
see you in hell battle for eternity.
there are worst things than being ashamed
you know you aren't about that life.
so, seek salvation.
know who you face to face with
a mask and gloves and gun are basic
who am I
they always have to learn the hard way.

like I don't got cocked and loaded all day
what a have to do tattoo killer on my forehead
if you make me pull it out
you couldn't be more dead.
wouldn't get away if you had four legs.
really wont.
am a laugh when I hear please don't?
just a john doe
stuffed in a suitcase.
right next to the sox and toothpaste
folded like lawn chairs.
your legs on your face
come find me 22 at the bottom of my soup.
AK on the roof
Place you in the basement.
Under the ceramic tile
And just light an incense once and a while
Who am I
Now that my jackets off
Its timid talks real soft
They know what those two bulges are
Under my white T on each side of where my pipe be
Cause I never had any patience for aggravation.
Any bitch statements.

Explode their faces.

Only the hood can relate.

Unfortunately, their killers in the making

A few wrong words and bullets chase men.

And don't really matter.

This is genocide.

Our own people against our people

Hating causing erasing

Of what is rightfully ours in the nation

Relax

I don't want to talk too much.
Might hear something that will mess up my mood
Consider the meanings in full.
No surprises just something predictable
The opposite to my perpendicular blues
Real cool smooth as fuck
Real food stewed and cut.
Dim the lights exactly how I like.
Lost in the night.
Nothing but matches.
To strike aromas that wake comas.
Just to put back in a daze
Forgetting the clock
Everything is right on time.
When you're feeling fine
Disappear like a soluble
When I'm in my solitude
I mystery to me unsolvable
At peace reject the bad vibes
That are intolerable.
But not perfect
Surely you noticed.

It's not worth it.
Working without purpose
Sitting thinking too long
Will you be there for me?
When my hairs are grey and reseeding
Cancer starts growing.
And the shouting like two trains collide.
Try to subside with the truer side.
Holding on to the little that's real
And subtract how I feel.
Walk away leaving the best part of me.
If it makes me weaker
To keep her
Our world like disaster-stricken city.
I must be alone so you can be with me.
I'm not trying to fight.
Let's find a lakeside.
Like the fantastic voyage
Forever takes courage

Young Again

They wanted to make us into Gods apprentice.
There's a lot of lessons
How to fight without a weapon
When life gets oppressive
Decode the message.
Celebrate your blessings.
And not impressed with a flashy necklace
Bottles in your section
Or how you dressing.
You could have it all then gone in a second.
I lived those night opening door without checking.
They were all welcome
Music blasting to drown the cussing
Inviting women we were crushing
The grill is going go and get you something.
All day we cooking.
Popping wheelies got a concussion.
When bud man came we crowd the cushions
Don't care if couldn't put in.
If I had it, you had it

Don't worry how your pocket looking.
All for one if ever confronted.
Couldn't tell us nothing.
The way we running.
Drinking like its Constituted
Made the convos more intuitive.
Every night same repetition
Life is better living.
The time I'm taking I bet against it.
If you think we stopping think again
Well known to what trouble is
Sometimes I wish I was young again.
The feeling of invincibility
No responsibility
Confident in all my abilities
Loving worlds amenities
If only age didn't come for me
I'd be running free until the lord come for me

Mirror Mirror

Who I compete with
Can't cheat with
First person I'm meeting.
Practice greetings
Fuss over neatness
Argue over who he is.
Is there any pleasing.
My misfortune sees it.
No smile I see fit.
Do it to hide weakness?
The weekends be the realest.
Just don't expose my secrets.
Talk about it.
But not know by many misunderstood
Held in safe keeping.
Not in my breathing
Even if was freezing.
Circles my mind when I'm sleeping.
Counting barely getting by the
Skin of my teeth is.
Black sheeping

Less needed

This color needs teaching

I don't know where to begin.

Mirror Mirror

This the vantage point to the soul

Sees all the pressures in whole.

Lifetime visual transformation enrolled.

Loophole to my control

Mental telephone

Inside of us all

Commit to that creole boy.

Running home back drops

Of mango trees

Dancing around fires

Mirror Mirror who shines brighter

Take on all fighters.

Do I strike you as a survivor?

Made by the best of fibers

Mirror Mirror

The greatest grand gesture

Made in the image of pharaohs and kings.

Can't forget my queens.

Wouldn't be anything without you on my team.

Mirror Mirror

Try to change the ideology.

Into False prophecies

Put us in categories.

Involved in criminology.

But they can't take what empowers me

No apologies

Yeah, I see I see.

For their atrocities

Unforgivable

Passed getting down on my knee

Limited resources

But say we do things out of greed.

Only I see what they can't see.

In the mirror

Love After Death

They say I was hardheaded.
But was knocking on deaths door
How could I listen?
Death wishes
Like premonitions.
In need of radical reform
The words get invasive.
Sight gets grated.
Follow me past gated graves end.
You can hear chanting enchantments
Their waiting.
Mind casted until the page ends.
Only quick action
Will allow safe passage.
It's all booby trapped in
You must see it before
It happens.
The trees and the skies
get clashed in.
The ground feels like ashes.
The closest you get
The farthest away you are.

In my mind like
thousands of envelopes
in a couple of draws.
Your not alone,
in the world of nocturnes
the wind on your back turns you.
The silence of crickets warns you.
If I was ever lost
it was because I held on to long,
to the things that were far and gone.
When asked I just shrugged it off
and portrayed I was strong.
At the same time sacrilegious
maybe I was counting wrong.
losing what I'm counting on
more and more
it's just continuous.
Fuck it what is going on.
Shoulders worn.
Heart is torn.
You are mine I am yours
mirage silhouettes
waiting for you in a large charrette.
Frightened without a blink.

But I could be the syndicate to
your wish.
Nights are sacred.
You can see it hear it in the pitch.
You were handpicked.
As the others withered on the vine.
The objection to your shrine.
The connection on either side of the
Twine.
In the middle of the turning of times
In turn you will find.
I may have the difficult of minds.
If only I could pause minutes for
Hours and rewind.
See the index and the guide.
I wouldn't be so obsessed of what
becomes of us when we die.
Just thankful you were there for the ride.

Vegas Nights

Initials on the cuff links
Shit that bust 6 off my hips
Puffing on something that stinks
Armani suits
Versace cologne drenched in
Moet on the Armoire
Would discuss some cars but that's a different song.
Just me and you and chafer
Marble floors
100-gallon tank in the walls
Glass figurines
Gold trimming on the mirrors
Dimond lace
She like the drank with the gold flakes
Dress long as a gown
It's going down.
With all this fashion may never show
May never know.
We both criminals
She ducts tape the work.
I use the same roll to tie you up.

Spend the night pressing our luck.
I bet on black she put it on red.
Got a full house she got a royal flush.
Now who want to fuck with us?
Ashes to ashes dust to dust
Got my team to left bad ass Keisha to the right.
Just came off a three-hour flight.
Feds already got the warrant typed.
You can lose your life on these Vegas nights.
What better way to walk away rolling the dice
7-11
Poolside at Caesars palace
Just imagine.
Sunny skies and warm pool waters
Tan line and umbrellas over us
The other in a vodka coconut
Trying not to be suspicious
Faces on television.
Ray bans under her sunhat
I had to grow a mustache.
Everybody want to be a boss.
But afraid to take a loss.
Maybe it's a lack of better cause.
Turning you back and wont shelter yours

I'm a blow it all before they change this king back to frog.

gone

Ain't no way I can right my wrongs

Fuckin Flip Flops

How far can you go with your eyes close?
Mama taught me how to pray.
So you'll never be far away
Skies the limit
And I never been on a plane
So just let me ride this wave

Float with the wishes and the lost ones
Oh, that thought is so insane
Remember when I thought rain,
were the lord's pain.
Zeus flying with lighting bolts in his hand.
Runway to the golden gates
followed by winged children singing Amen.
Where everybody gets in free
but gotta be a G.

Mama taught me how to pray
So you'll never be far away
Sky's the limit
and I never been on a plane.

So just let ride this wave.

Got to experience it for myself,
when I get to Tsa tell them to pick my flops up
Their fucking self
Will Mufasa tell me I am king.
Or will I have nightmares of monsters on the wings,
and doesn't get hijacked by someone crazed.
or a hundred of snakes
Hope I get premonitions like Alex did,
if we are going to crash.
Think I seen snoop behind the wheel,
someone hide the stash.
There's a man with a red cape,
carrying us on his back.

Mama taught me how to pray
So you'll never be far away
Sky's the limit .
And I never been on a plane.
So just let me ride this wave.

A Lot More

I was getting around.
When I should be around more
Love to see my niggas make it.
Throw the ball off the back board!
Riding four deep just me and my boys
That was living.
Laughing about similar problems
Never had an issue getting dollars.
My girl seen me pull up.
Said slow down before you get locked up.
Even worse shot up.
Wondering if my dreams are
Worth losing my life for
Moe deep in depression over a loss
And loss her
Little brother defending his own.
And got caught up.
One of peoples did three.
The other did five
Grandma watching flames.
Take everything she worked hard for
Our DJ in and out the funeral homes

Man, we have to pray for all us
The feeling is unexplainable.
Couldn't be mad in a world so hate able.
Bb king Eric Clapton on the mind
More seats than mouths on the table
This time
Demons chasing me want to see me sweat.
Is why I aint slow down yet.
No more shorts because I'm doing my best.
Who's next.
Reveal the scars imprinted on my flesh.
Rather who it's what.
A lot of fucks but not one to give
But they watch at a close distance.
When I have nothing

I was getting around when.
I should be around more.
I was living.
should have appreciated life more.
finding myself in slides
than shoes a lot more
sharpen my mind.
with sharp tools

teaching instead of looking
to see a lot more
a lot more
I name becomes no definitive.
Love can't be explained at its earliest form.
It's presented by its mirror.
Of affections suitable
Love is beauty usable.
Unrefusable
Highly disputable
Confusable passion
Is what we do it for lose it for?
Distance makes you feel it more.

MCBYL Money Can't Buy You Love.

This time it's Different.
Ignore the differing.
Not interested in the literary
I was suffering from ignorance.
Now my heart the temperature of a refrigerant.
The bickering turned to gibberish.
Man, I was belligerent.
All this confusion I was configuring.
A lot of shit I should have been bigger than.
Left you with unfinished business.
Didn't mean to let you fill it in
couldn't see when the feeling went.
Damaged ceilings and crooked floors
And bent corridors.
The house has no home when you are gone.
Aint no mending this broken heart.
Just let Al Green elaborate.
Love on the first sight
First second into my heartrate.
Schoolmate to roommate
Gravitate I'm the astronaut you be the Martian.
The bad one I be sergeant.

Jane and the Tarzan
Loyal servant I'll be the Spartan.
I promise to keep a spark in
Listen to every word when you are talking.
Can't stop calling.
Just waiting for you to walk in

This Carrera sits two I need you to move.
Don't need no space there's plenty of room.
I dream of you let me prove its true
Haunted by scents of your perfume.
Buy anything you choose!
But money can't buy you love
I tried diamonds and gold.
Louie Vuitton tickets Pari
Benzes and fenty
Embarrassed that you my enemy

And She said it's your loss
Took the mat at the front door.
Because you're not.
No kisses in the seat we should
Be living.
Sink full of dishes we can be eating

Hope you know how to wash and fold
You going to be freezing.
And all the dust going to
Effect your breathing.
Don't even think about the
Nights of love and where we shared.
Our feelings
And when your home reading this
Maybe you'll know.
What its like to be alone.
Prideful for all the wrong reasons.
She wrote be this letter on Friday.
Said she was leaving.
Slipped under my pillowcase.
Gave me the weekend.
Too hardheaded to feel it.
Now I'm staring dead flowers in a vase.
From my last mistakes
Bag packed for days.
Knew I would never see it.
Its still to hard to believe it
Found this the first night.
She was by my side when I was sleeping.

Get More

The devil built a house on my back
Took out 30-year mortgage.
And he pays it.
I wear sunglasses in the dark.
So,i don't see the shadows that he lay in.
These hallways are the streets.
And the steps are getting steep.
Is it me?
Or can these walls speak?
And the wino on the corner warning
Of what he sees
Hell, fire plagues and bumps.
You gotta live.
When squeeze make sure you get
Every drop
Got juice but make some pie too.
Keep making them calls and he'll
Find you.
I'm marching with the greatness.
Hell been on earth so try not to
Embrace it.

Sometimes to get to the top you
Must break the foundation.
Kick down doors.
Find your own ladder.
Piss in the wind if you need your
Reign to happen faster.

Don't worry about those fumes.
Breath it in
We all sip out the same chalice
Like Jesus did
A holy elicitor that flickers fixtures
This could have been a scripture.
Kings burned books and painted.
Their own pictures.
All I need is a page for that swisher.
Wait while I twist up.
They want to know how much.
The wristwatch worth
About one night of that wrist work
Let me know the ship cost.
If they catch me, you know how long.
I'm a sit for
Chains linked like the neck of a Pitbull.

All I know is I have to get more
Get More
Evil surround these big bucks
This is what I live for
Instinctively we are linked between.
Good and bad
Truth and lies.
Life or death
I just close my eyes and tat names
That are holy to me inside my flesh.
They want to see the relativity.
But there's no cut fold or symmetry.
That can match this energy.
Spoken through calligraphy.
I share my soul with this world ambiguously.
We share the same fears.
Questions unanswered like their begging
Us to dare.
No reactions to actions as if the truth
Was never there.
Thinking we are not aware.

In my heart

Forever in my mind only you
The pieces of my life go away with you.
Flashing scenes bring me back to you.
Tossing and turning
Disrupting my heart
Lights are twirling I continue to fight.
If only I could heal like wolverine
Everyday feels like Halloween.
Demons hopped up on caffeine.
Sweating the shirt off my back
Burning from the suns beam
So, guarded with what's to be.
Mood up and down like a trampoline.
No rope levitation
Or am I the one that my minds betraying?
Past anything I could medicate with
Negative meditation
Trapped within too difficult to break.
In a paranoid state even if you can't relate
Keep me safe keep them away.
Or is peace out of my reach?

Will I ever sleep?
What lies beneath is a leash.
That stole my away speech.
From my breath and the beat
Cause if it was up to me.
You would never leave.
Forever in my heart alone in the dark
That's when we are never apart.
Until we meet again at the end of the day
This is where my heart will stay.

Make It

Time and pressure make diamonds.
Spread my words across the pages
Like Michael Angelo's collages
To the Gods is
When I'm gone They going to
Wrap me like a pharaoh.
Images that bring cold sweats
In the darkness
The silence echoes
In underground caves
When I'm talking
Clutching crosses
As footprints creek
And burn up the varnish.
Wishing on shooting stars is
Give me the comet

Some days a barely make it
But wont stop till I made it
Admiration in my name

When they say it
Adding to my savings
Shoe box is what the safe is
Till life shape shifts
Even though its laws
That I'm breaking
Highly motivated
Aint nothing to play with

I need the whole building.
My name on the top floor
Parking
I would never sell my soul.
For something to accomplish
Just out work the demons
Till they jobless
God gives and takes.
Same way he tested if job lives.
You don't know
How far is when your only means?
Is walking.
Getting up when your reputation
Is tarnished.
Need a rocket ship.

To put me in my placement
I swear I need patience.
Feels like forever waiting.
Music is my rock.
I am David.
Goliath is hatred.
Try not to preach.
But we surrounded by
Energy
Something you feel but
Can't see.
It's basis where my love?
Is founded.
And where I find my peace when
All my thoughts are clouded.

Trapped Words

The smallest thing can spark a flame.

Old unresolved issues can cloud your brain.

Emotional memories lead to the decisions you make.

Nothing can take away the pain.

So, you're sipping and twisting multiple times a day.

Like bullet wounds covered with just band aids

Paranoid with the hurt can't move the any way

Losing connections, it's seeming strange.

Lost in the shame.

Never in one place to long

Bottled up rage.

Nervousness stomach filled with razor blades.

Lips trembling the words can't stay.

Letting it out even though the scars have aged.

Now your screaming surprised by your voices range

Tears stream and stain

Your hearts racing feeling faint.

Letting go all you have even if they're not to blame.

The person in front of you is not the same.

Calling them by another name

My mind took the place of my heart.

Some say I'm confused.

Steal and use do with them as I choose.

Guilt them with their fear to lose

Trapped them with word like

....

She ain't taking it for nothing.

All your demons confronted.

Challenging you with your running

It was always something.

This tough exterior

Was no match for life's superior?

Of dumping and cutting fucking what you wanted

Or was it love?

The feeling is haunting.

Your time is coming.

So, take it out on anyone.

Cornered in a ring.

Knives in your back

Mornings in black

replacing the facts

maybe I'm too attached.
cause I'm about snap.
as they look and they laugh
I should have been left where I was at
To a whole different map
Away from your cap
Put up crazy stats
Don't know why put up with that
Repeating the past
Rather look through the glass
Leaving my footprints in the grass
We are something that could be never had
This end will be the last

Love With

This not what you expected.
Stay ten toes.
Same morals that I left with
Everyone got something to say.
Something gotta give.
I'm hardly away and they still want me to stay.
It doesn't take nothing for me to go.
My bags packed I'm already moving on the low
I done made it through the snow.
Looking forward to the glow
Its better the less you know.
She wants us to grow.
I think its best we don't.
Those plans I don't see them anymore.
Hope you find what you're looking for.
I been looking at the door.
Trying to deal with the problems at the core
If it was about commitment
I was never sure.
Staring at the shoes you used
To walk all over me

Those apologies you can keep.
Try to play me like I was weak.
Like I needed you more than I needed me
I know what I said I know what I done
And what I felt
Me and that other lady is doing well.
Looking forward to who going to tell
Mine work for mine
She twerks for time.
She doesn't need no wine and dine.
Not penny pinching
You got your match I'm that nigga.
Raised to hustle.
Don't worry what you have to do
To make this paper we can celebrate later.
Dance if you want to
All these niggas want to
Got bands go ahead and come through
Do anything you want to
She said there's nothing I won't do.
You going to make me break the safe
Won't be evening until we wake.
I done came a long way.
From getting beat with branches

Buy any whip I want.
Wasn't giving no direction.
Had to make my own moves.
They hated the discretion.
And rumored about my preference.
Thick, slim brown or yellow
But I love those rough diamonds.
That were raised inside the ghetto.
Ass like jello
Mood on melo
She rocks the retros over the stilettos.
Two-piece new weave
She said if you balling you going to have to show me.
Got women trying to fight me.
Men trying to find me.
She made like ten stacks like last week.
Blew it all on her kids.
Everything on time where she lives.
Her mom's good she respects the grind.
But she misunderstood.
Been the best of times and the worst of times.
Trying to blueprint it out.
With a 380 in her purse at church
Her body was a gift and a curse.

Even copped some work.

4.0 gpa puts the books first.

On a mission no time to be cooking in the kitchen

She taught to be the one out fishing.

Remember

Laying on the cold floor by the door
Hard enough still couldn't hold on to a job
Going far walking past their cars
When I had one, I slept in it.
Being talked about like I didn't get it.
With the struggle I was finished
Started with an ounce.
Got rid of two sevenths.
Copped another half.
Put rest in the stash.
Broke it down to nine bags of 20.
That's 180
Repeat until did a full turn around.
That's 360
I aint doing no cuffing fuck you pay me.
Take away the 150 for the reup.
Put away 210.
Had to do it again for a quarter.
That's 600

Was short 30.
Brought it back with interest.
In ten minutes
Connect threw me a P
That was everything I needed.
To get off my feet

Moved in with 3 bands.
Put my room in the back.
Turned a 2 to a 4
Goons at the door
Only people we are trusting been here before
My niggas like me brothers
My brothers Love ya
Could get a lecture from any of our mothers.
Shout out to the OG he showed me the hustle
Out of town more than a trucker
Nobody we had to front for
Keep each other humble.
Never Roswell where we came from

Now I'm maxing the dash with no buckle.

My words could touch you.

My balls next to the nuzzle.

It's all I have to confront you.

No more broken noses

and bloody knuckles

The knives in your back

Come from ones that hug you

Close

Shells will seal your fate.
Can you imagine doctors trying?
To seal your face
Stomach grumbling
Thinking of the last meal you ate
Now I'm picking off your plate.
Lord please don't take me back to this place
Night that I wanted to cry like a baby.
But prayed like a nun.
If these thought proceeds
I will decrease my chances to succeed.
My dreams turning into nightmares.
No light but the moon through the shade
Counting on a breeze like a blessing sent
In cool air
A slight howl thinking you was there
Come and get this money and fame.
We can make a fair exchange.
Take my hand you will be made
Fighting back the rage
Let me relieve you pain.

A rapid knocking waiting for
The clear of the day
As I fall deeper and deeper into the dark
What price can you purchase
the soul of a man?
Crammed into one choice.
Heard by one voice.
Nevermore
Looking to the sky asking lord why
What I feel aint your presence
Chased by an essence.
At the point of my stressing
What I need is a blessing
Send me a blessing.
Direct from the heavens
Like a hundred million volts

Streets are getting hot.
I weather whatever the weather brings.
Followed by dark feathered wing.
From where they never say a thing and
Your never seen again.
Tears extinguish my pain.
Try to distinguish my desire for change.

Lair will always remain.
They always saying names.
Pictures say a thousand words.
My heart says a million more.
The past creates a timeline.
It's what happens now that writes its
Now and every moment
Will be lived with no regrets.
I am hoping if I make a mistake, it's in the sand
And my tears wash away in the sea.
If I ever make it to my dreams
Don't let my castle go along with it.

Believe

Second wind I'm a need a second pen.
When there's seconds to win
I'm the one they bring.
Beatings worse than Mexicans
It's not about a thing but those dollars
Holla
Stay proper.
You going to prop up like undertaker.
Can't stop us.
Flyest thing since a saucer
Red dotter terminator John Conner
Maze of stairs to walk up.
Trying to find the doors they talk of
With a whole lot of
But it's a set up I've been set up.
What is it you believe?
Do they not bleed?
Is that not enough to see?
Things aren't as they seem.
Caught in a web of dreams.
Understand even the blind reads.

They see what's in between.
The collision is extreme.
Tension at a zillion degree
When realized the reality received?
Won't break can't fall.
Wont stray will brawl.
Stay woke even odds.
Have hope life's hard.
Connect content.
Shit is dying at arm's length.
Only way to progress.
Is to destroy what you think you know.
Until there's nothing left
Stand by my word until my last breath.
Shit got me stressed.
Herbs gives my mind rest.
Peace was the conquest.
But the treaty beyond wrecked.
You don't know I'm the bomb yet.
Overslept in-depth effect to reflect.
If frog would have leapt without long legs
The chicken or the egg
The oven or the bread
The abyss has one wish.

A never-ending glitch.

Which side are you with?

The here and the now or the air and the clouds

Are you listening

All mighty God are you listening.
Don't tell me nothing.
These niggas or these bitches
Point to the millions.
Where it's at and I will go go get it
Heavy foot on the pavement
Go the whole ground shaking.
Just bring back to my mamas baking
She was battling look how far she made it
Keep me in your graces.
I just have make it
Iron every dollar before I tie my laces.
Grew up a bastard.
Don't know how many times
my father drove right pass us.
Spent all my time getting plastered.
Getting a little attention I was flattered
Room was clattered.
Women was letting me in like I had the password.
Should've wrapped it up like a hazard.

Acting like it didn't matter.
Boy, girl then another boy.
Life caught up to me faster.
But there's no way I'm going backwards
Slowed the recklessness.
I was on the way to disaster.
They are looking up to me.
They going to need some answers.
In and out of the psych ward
Must have thought I was finished.
Left me with all these children.
I can't blame her everyone gives in
Even eve ate the fruit that was forbidden
We all deserve fulfillment.
But I'm back in the building.
Driven under the conditions.
To provide a life sufficient
I have to do anything.
No time to second guess my decisions.
My conviction put me in position.
To beat the opposition
Until they distant
Warning the competition
Like I was a physician

Make them disappear like I'm a magician.
If want to get technical
I got tools I'm a technician.
Don't want to be forgiven.
Don't want to be excused.
Don't need your approval.
I was excluded.
The world had me subdued.
I just widen my margin.
Do what I have to do.
Never beg or bargain
This is how I rule.

Makings of a Villain

Born winner losing fast.
Studied on his own development was last
Smallest one in the class
Quiet so he walked without a pass
Hiding behind books of the past
Fascinated with wars and the imagination he has.
On the walk home he's picking out the trash
Found a camo bag.
Put in everything he loves.
If he leaves there's no looking back
Dressed in all black with a fitted cap.
Home wasn't a place he could get a laugh.
In need of a dentist figured he was mad
No role model maybe all he needed was his dad.
Gone but he was glad.
Those beating were getting bad.
Picking fights to cover up the bruises he had.
Wearing dark shades to mask the fear.
Vowed to never shed a tear.
Confused by all the voices he can hear.

Big loud headphone so he didn't care.
Caught with a weapon.
So, they sent him to juvenile detention.
Said maybe there was a problem with attention.
This will teach a well needed lesson.
Formed a group with the same prospective
These are the makings of a villain.
Groomed for disaster.
Passion for danger
Criminal behavior
Less favored
Not a friend or a neighbor
Willingly sins of labor.
Lost and gone living for that paper.
Chasing dreams, he wasn't made for
Explosive anger
The kid they gave up.
Turned his back on the savior.
These are the Makings of villain.

Luggage and Shovels

Amazing music got feeling like a superhero.

Rich in your heart this moment got you stupid zeros.

Capturing emotion creating a vibe

Mind of a ruler in nations

Uplifting my soul's pride

Stoic in mind

With a personalized deed

Between me myself and I

Cutting the breeze

This is home the only place I got left to go.

I see the notes.

Mention me three times and I am there

Ready for what's near.

Shadowy figures rolling in the night.

I'm a member.

The end where the master appears.

I can't be any clearer.

Understand every element like the last air bender.

I'm no thug or no gangster.

Don't say everything I think of

More like the bigger picture
When nothing going right
But the sun still shining bright.
What's supposed to help is sucking out your life
Nerves at its height
Trusting no one
Looking at them twice
Making something out of nothing
On my last hinges
Voices got my ear ringing.
Behind the exterior there's a grimace
I don't know how but I be falling sometime.
Can't hold up.
Its anarchy lone solider
This will never blow ova
You couldn't tell my vision if you had your own show bruh
I'm not here to sympathize.
Its all luggage and shovels
You can take a nose dive in a puddle
A hail of brainstorms
I could funnel a tunnel.
Chilling half the time like trumpets and drumming
It's nothing

Foolish Gold

Some hearts are not meant to be played with
9 rights by the keys to the truck
From me to you for us
This is more about her.
I would pay to watch her strut
Even offer to pay so we could fuck.
Only shame is if I do it in a rush.
On video uncut
You know I'm from the streets run up.
Not looking for no love
You can have what you desire
One life in the game, watch out for the liars.
I played a few lost windows and tiers.
Never thought it could make them snakes.
Nothing you can do to make me stay.
The heart still searches any way.
The trouble begins at the end of the horizon.
The footsteps are getting closer.
I'm steady looking over my shoulder.
Thinking the devil is getting closer.

I caught in a fire.
The smoke billows.
Then explodes as the wind blows.
You don't have to say anything
She already knows.
Been watching you from the get-go.
She aint no hoe
If her eyes could speak you would already know
You not leaving here alive.
Its not what you did between her thighs.
But what you did to her mind
She not even gonna cry.
Enticing her with more lies
She is coming for all that you got.
The only way to deal with the shock.
The floors crackling.
Any minute you drop.
You don't know when to stop.
The paint drips from the walls
Exposing you for who you are
The light always finds its way to the dark.
You can see the rain from a far.
The gasoline trails back to the car
You thought this ride was cheap.

Hells gates is open.

Last thing you'll hear is the click of her feet.

Not even the chills will set you free.

The coldest side of me

The only one that was there if you ever need.

Wouldn't drip off a chuckle if you plead.

I should have known.

You were just fool's gold

No Thing Else

I don't need nothing else.
I can't see nothing else.
I don't feel nothing else.
I don't need fucking help.
It calls me calling me.
She tells my fortune through the cards.
Fell my heart going further and beyond
Watch my dreams from a far.
Still believing in these stars
Staring at the pictures that it draws
Losing track of where we are
Looking for the keys to the knob
Sew my soul with your yarn.
Wrap my body keep me warm.
Shelter me from the storm
My mind sharp like a sword
And at peace during wars
Alert me with a chord.
When it's time to be yours
And say goodbye to this world.
Probably wouldn't mind if it was dark forever

Take the sun from the sky miss it never.
Broken but at night I feel together.
Skin develops leather.
Heart the blender
Air the propeller
Ice in the drink that compels ya
I'm around the most and feel left out.
The more noise is usually when I check out.
Can't connect with the joy sought out.
Always looking for solitude
That my best route
Then I'm back on my altitude
To get a breath out
Confirming the doubt
Late night calling ladies
You know what that's bout.
Blow her back out.
And light some weed.
Before we both pass out.

FLEX

Be strong hold your head up.
The best is yet to come.
You're going to get there.
And when you do just flex
Now flex now flex.
Your grave danger
I want you out this world.
Like a space ranger
This the game changer
Got more moves.
Then black ranger
Hockey mask
Gloves with knives
Like Vega
Don't be mad be proud at
A playa
Like the bougie type
Prada head full of curls
Diamonds and pearls
Heels and some furs

Call it a required taste.
I retire fakes.
Let me check them.
When they out of place
Move blindly.
Drip was timely.
Created a prosoma.
That seemed to unbothered.
And make distance.
Hoping to make you.
Nonexistent
Separate should have waved.
At your persistence
Something stayed.
I was craving the
Drinking
Forgetting days
Nights are better played.
But I'm the best of the best
Can't put me with the rest
Wont rest
till I get it off my chest
I got weight to press.
Now flex now flex.

Now flex now flex.
Humble but eager
Wall street demeanor
Get it you know they need you
You know they do.
Now flex now flex.
Now flex now flex.
You got it and did.
Something with it
Trouble is something.
You must live with
When you hustle and you driven
Staking every dollar
Earning every cent
Nothing was given.
Nothing
Type to tie strings to triggers.
Wrap them around doorknobs.
Your gone.
Acting like you impressive
Fake as unicorn impressions
Like you the only one
With yours on
Do you understand?

The knowledge I'm professing.
Pledge legion to weapon
Slid through like socks.
On waxed wood
Head on plaque wood
Would you be around?
If you were where I stood
Vipers in the garden
Got to watch where you walk.
Riding mongoose
They bite and they mad.
When it's not you
Shit is useless stuck like hot glue.
Travel in my shoe
Before deciding what is true
The devil is a lie.
I carried many that died.
Despite all the efforts I tried
Dispute the giving of
Lesser time
You aint loss your mind
Till you see a baby in
Casket
Got me running hot missing a

Gasket
Prayed for things that could.
Never happen.
Real definition of tragic
Look at all the pain I mastered.
Shit is Ticking bomb.
Truck going 80 while.
Its backing till its crashing
I would never sell another.
Thing
If you could keep drugs away
From my lil bro and keep him
Under your wind
Write forever if the story.
Had no ending or
Place another bet and take.
The odds against him
Study your word to put a
Second guess in
You the messiah
Spread around the message.
Bring warmth to the coldest.
Of fleshes

Comfort in knowing.

I take comfort in my own special things
Like red roses and knowing where I'm going
And seeing you before my eyes are closing.
There when its opening
I take comfort in knowing.
That my kids are well feed
Before they sleep in their own beds
My bills paid even if it's a little late
Gas full and heard that squeaking it make.
Some money in the bank few gees
And stank green in the fonto to take a break.
I take comfort in knowing.
There's a spring after the winter.
As long as I can call you hear that you are good.
Quiet day in the hood.
My waves spinning and my team focused on winning.
Clean clothes to switch up when I want wanna
Doing right by others feeling my karma
Stay true to your energy.
Showing respect and honor

I take comfort in knowing.
Every day I wake there a new way.
And possibilities are flowing.
No weapons against me shall prosper.
Little bottle of holy water
Before I give my problems to the father
Been through the most.
I take comfort in knowing.
That what don't kill me will make me stronger
This march has no band.
This drummer has no hands.
Lights is off there no fans.
The flutes echo until it gone.
The tambourine shaking something wrong.
My heart orchestrates the loneliest of songs.
Just coordinate the screams
Lump in my throat preventing to talk at all.
Close my eyes try to escape all he pains that I saw.
Who she is to me on the tip of my tongue.
I take comfort in knowing.
You'll forever live through your sons.

The Introduction

Somebody always watching him.
Like his name was George Washington
Greed enough to make you want to sin.
All for a taste of those grapes
After laboring
It's never enough.
Seconds left couple jabs with the right.
And you still aint winning this fight.
But you been preparing all your life.
Crawled walked then ran.
You gave it your all.
Said more the less you talked.
To be the exception to the rule
They are expecting you to lose
If I catch you watch what I do
If only you could see my truth
My tears are gateway.
With one drop we can communicate
Same language same vision
Same anguish same mission

I prayed then asked for forgiveness.
I gave believed in his existence.
Don't know how long the list is.
Or even if he's listening.
Probably won't get it.
This is my world sky faded the sun fell
The earth burned until it was missing.
Would stars have a reason to illuminate.
Muddy shoes backyard
Basketball with crates
Rusty chains bikes with no brakes
Shots and sirens
You can't excuse this place.
New projection with the same exceptions
Got to stay protected.
Twilight zone you to heaven
Breath is a blessing.
Waking up and I pissed in the bed again.
Do you know who's ring your stepping in?
Big stepper
disciplined proper eating eutectic.
oversized hand me downs
what I'm dressing in
I want it more ate fruit planted the core.

Shoplifting kicked out the store.
Hungry stood outside of the door.
Popping ignitions and rode by the boys
Flipped mattresses ransacked the draws.
Even if I'm not eye to eye.
I'm standing tall.
Built for the battle.
I want it all.

Pull Up

I been absent at your doors lord.
Two wrong don't make a right.
But can you hear those bikes?
Flag wrap my gat.
Yeah, I'm strapped.
Crazy as I want to be
I was speeding can't you tell
Road smokey the tires smell.
Hail to the bosses and the hustlers
Choppers and the customers
All the ladies loving us.
Pop a perky laying naked under comforters
Got her repping where I'm coming from
Clip full gotta use it.
Gotta do it
Popping like a southern dance
In my east coast stance
There's nothing casual.
If you see me with them then they family
10 out 10 fuck a friend.
20 years bled and shed tears.

You know who you are.

There's no need for explanations.

Shout out to my Haitians.

Always odds against us

We all we got.

Only trust in God.

There is no prayer in sight.

No not tonight

Have to get my paper right.

Only way out this life

Don't even see the light.

Or really now you see me now.

I'm the one they been talking about

All around town

Rocks under my tongue

Money in my boots

Watch your mouth when you speak about our crew

Cause we pull up.

Cook up.

Cane with that sugar

Count a hundred stacks.

And I look up.

We believe in working hard.

Thank you, GOD

Point of view

Wrapped and bound me on my journey.
I don't even know where I'm at
Tail wind of a tornado
Nothing will last.
In my path confronting functions
Every decision is rash.
Punished for bluffing so studied the math
Numbers lie when you relive the past.
Trying to pull rain from the dirt.
Is a heavy-hearted forecast.
Against the best of me
Handle the points my seat set.
No hand to hand
Watching the game as it progresses
Place your bets my streets next.
Many die before being let free
Is rap or poetry I can't between
You all got shit fucked up.

This not me hiding or crying.
Trying or buying
More like a sign of me climbing.
New attention openers
Strips like Jupiter
Broken down molecular formular.
No sensor or editor
Solo executor
How can not see me all of me
Open wound like a hammer to a knife
Back turn they made advances to my life.
Used to drinking with a spike.
Know well henny was my hell.
Took half of what I had to give.
Head in the sink circling
The drain with no one to blame.
You know how to get down.
Don't make a sound.
What goes around comes back around?
If it comes up, then it comes down
Stay low in town.
Moving like the world renowned
The man with the crown
Its just my emotional truth

What my soul forces to use
Don't let this world closen your view.
Evolved from what's told to do
Smokey barrels
I know when to shoot.

Island Thang

She gonna get down on it.
Like Kool and the gang.
Aint new to the change.
Everything we do is strange.
We don't do no strings.
Attraction is I knew the game.
No pillow talking exchanging names.
Big on flavor she wants me now and later.
Save the day to stay away.
Can't go all week.
Meet me at the beach.
Its Wednesday
Even a camel knows kissing on your toes.
Chocolate but her skin is gold.
From the November to the sprang
She my Island thang

She my Island thang
She my island thang
She my island thang

I got Haitians in Miami
Making plays like Dan Marino
I knew when I see you.
We'd be more than just aquatintist is
You know what this is.
Doing business with a kang
Listen out for my ring.
Thought benefiting was a better thang.
Now we like more the best of friends.
Real island bae
She my island queen
Showing what she bangs

I'm into it

You lunch me to a boss
I'm straight out the wildlife.
I celebrate with some conch meat.
Inside some sauce and side of wild rice
I'm chilling on a recliner.
Floating on a geyser
With a pack of rottweilers
And the chains are off.
Native to the land
The 45s are the bow and arrows.
The bucks are the tomahawks.
Those graves I did them shallow.
To get my point across
Throw yall all in
It's a bargain fertilizer for the farming.
Take the pieces and birth a Frankenstein.
Hunt for riches that were never mine
Tell them it's like wings in the wind.
It will always fly.

The body follow the mind.
When its thinking wises
Between the opioids fentanyl dope mix
The city stuck like a polaroid.
Ready to end it all.
Even the corporate got a nose twitch.
Its important of my potence
Souls are marketable for the potion.
Dimensions are getting crossed.
Good intentions are steady lost.
My vision is tinted I can't see my image.
On the mirrors on the at all
Standing alone like I walk on walls.
Still about my pyramids
I told you that I'm into it
She only loves for inches is
But I fell in love with money.
Felling like we intimate
Go hard so its continuous
Trunk full say prayer.
Then I go out and get this shit
If I get pulled over
Tonight's news going to be interesting.
Hopefully you can see what we are envisioning.

Chasing a trophy without witnesses
All I need is a empresses.
Pass it down to my princes and my princesses.
Security on the tower
Only for the Familia
They will kill ya
In this villa
surrounded clear water and pillars.

Made in the USA
Columbia, SC
27 May 2024

0d89c599-f074-4909-97a6-08bb7517290cR01